“Dare
to
live
the
life
you’ve
always
wanted.”

Gros
BOIS & CHARBONS
Détail
VINS - LIQUEURS

BAINS

8

5 BIS
JAZZ

BAINS
PIGALLE

GALERIE VIVIENNE

TS
MICRO

LE PURE CAFE

P

PASSAGE des PANORAMAS

RESTAURANT
New
KASHMIR
Gastronomie Indienne
New KASHMIR
AMI

LIVRES
LIBRAIRIE PAUL VULIN

12
PASSAGE JOUFFROY
10
HOTEL RONC

1846

PASSAGE - VERDEAU
PASSAGE VERDEAU
CONDUISANT
FAUBOURG MONTMARTRE

Photographies
anciennes
ESTAMPES

18e Arrt
PLACE
ÉMILE GOUDEAU

RUE
CARCEL

18e Arrt
RUE
JOSEPH
DE MAISTRE
1754 - 1821
AUTEUR CONTRE REVOLUTIONNAIRE
BAR
AMSTEL
BIERE
RESTAURANT

Burn like

CPSIA information can be obtained
at www.ICGtesting.com
Printed in the USA
BVHW050806110319
542311BV00023B/1402/P

9 780368 385346